SOUP RECIPES

A SOUP COOKBOOK FILLED WITH DELICIOUS SOUP RECIPES FOR ALMOST EVERY TYPE OF SOUP FOR EVERY SEASON

By
BookSumo Press
Copyright © by Saxonberg Associates

Published by
BookSumo Press, a DBA of Saxonberg Associates
http://www.booksumo.com/

ABOUT THE AUTHOR.

BookSumo Press is a publisher of unique, easy, and healthy cookbooks.

Our cookbooks span all topics and all subjects. If you want a deep dive into the possibilities of cooking with any type of ingredient. Then BookSumo Press is your go to place for robust yet simple and delicious cookbooks and recipes. Whether you are looking for great tasting pressure cooker recipes or authentic ethic and cultural food. BookSumo Press has a delicious and easy cookbook for you.

With simple ingredients, and even simpler step-by-step instructions BookSumo cookbooks get everyone in the kitchen chefing delicious meals.

BookSumo is an independent publisher of books operating in the beautiful Garden State (NJ) and our team of chefs and kitchen experts are here to teach, eat, and be merry!

INTRODUCTION

Welcome to *The Effortless Chef Series*! Thank you for taking the time to purchase this cookbook.

Come take a journey into the delights of easy cooking. The point of this cookbook and all BookSumo Press cookbooks is to exemplify the effortless nature of cooking simply.

In this book we focus on Soup. You will find that even though the recipes are simple, the taste of the dishes are quite amazing.

So will you take an adventure in simple cooking? If the answer is yes please consult the table of contents to find the dishes you are most interested in.

Once you are ready, jump right in and start cooking.

— BookSumo Press

TABLE OF CONTENTS

ANY ISSUES? CONTACT US

If you find that something important to you is missing from this book please contact us at info@booksumo.com.

We will take your concerns into consideration when the 2nd edition of this book is published. And we will keep you updated!

— BookSumo Press

Legal Notes

COMMON ABBREVIATIONS

cup(s)	C.
tablespoon	tbsp
teaspoon	tsp
ounce	oz.
pound	lb

*All units used are standard American measurements

Chapter 1: Easy Soup Recipes

Canadian Ginger and Maple Sweet Potato Curry Soup

Ingredients

- 5 C. chicken broth
- 2 large sweet potatoes, peeled and cut into cubes
- 2 C. baby carrots
- 1 onion, chopped
- 1 tsp red curry powder
- 3/4 tsp ground cinnamon
- 1/2 tsp ground ginger
- 1 C. half-and-half
- 2 tbsp real maple syrup
- Salt and ground black pepper to taste

Directions

- In a slow cooker, mix together the chicken broth, sweet potatoes, baby carrots, onion, red curry powder, cinnamon and ground ginger.
- Set the slow cooker on Low and cook, covered for about 7 hours.

- Remove from the heat and keep aside to cool slightly.
- In a blender, add the mixture in batches and pulse till smooth.
- Return the pureed soup into the slow cooker.
- Stir in the half-and-half, maple syrup, salt and pepper.
- Set the slow cooker on High and cook, covered for about 20 minutes.

Amount per serving 9

Timing Information:

Preparation	20 m
Cooking	7 h 20 m
Total Time	7 h 40 m

Nutritional Information:

Calories	159 kcal
Fat	3.5 g
Carbohydrates	28.9g
Protein	3.3 g
Cholesterol	13 mg
Sodium	667 mg

* Percent Daily Values are based on a 2,000 calorie diet.

ALTERNATIVE CAULIFLOWER CURRY SOUP II

Ingredients

- 1 tbsp olive oil
- 1/2 onion, sliced
- 3 carrots cut into 1/2-inch slices
- 1/2 red bell pepper, sliced
- 3 cloves garlic, peeled
- 1 head cauliflower, chopped
- 1 (32 fluid oz.) container chicken stock
- 2 tbsp yellow curry powder
- 1 tbsp butter
- 4 dashes hot sauce
- Salt and ground black pepper to taste

Directions

- In a large pan, heat the oil on medium heat and sauté the onion, carrots, red bell pepper and garlic for about 5-10 minutes.
- Add the cauliflower and chicken broth and bring to a boil.
- Cook for about 10 minutes.

- Remove from the heat and with a hand blender blend till smooth.
- Return the pan on low heat and stir in the curry powder, butter, hot sauce, salt and pepper.
- Simmer for about 15 minutes.
- Serve hot.

Amount per serving 8

Timing Information:

Preparation	15 m
Cooking	30 m
Total Time	45 m

Nutritional Information:

Calories	75 kcal
Fat	3.8 g
Carbohydrates	9.6g
Protein	2.5 g
Cholesterol	4 mg
Sodium	403 mg

* Percent Daily Values are based on a 2,000 calorie diet.

VEGAN SPLIT PEAS AND CARROTS CURRIED

Ingredients

- 3 tbsp olive oil
- 1/4 C. lemon juice
- 8 cloves garlic, minced
- 3 carrots, sliced
- 2 white onions, sliced
- 6 stalks celery, sliced
- 10 C. water
- 8 cubes chicken bouillon
- 2 C. dried split peas
- 1 tbsp Italian seasoning
- 1 tsp ground cumin
- 1 tbsp salt
- 1 tbsp ground black pepper
- 1/2 tsp cayenne pepper
- 4 tsp curry powder

Directions

- In a large pan, heat the olive oil on medium heat and cook the lemon juice, garlic, carrots, onions and celery for about 20 minutes.
- Transfer the vegetables and their juices into a bowl and refrigerate to cool slightly.
- In a blender, add the mixture ad pulse till smooth.
- In a large pan, dissolve the chicken bouillon cubes in the water on medium heat.
- Add the vegetable puree and bring to a boil.
- Stir in the split peas, Italian seasoning, cumin, salt, black pepper, cayenne pepper and curry powder.
- Reduce the heat to medium-low and simmer for about 45 minutes.

Amount per serving 20

Timing Information:

Preparation	20 m
Cooking	1 h 5 m
Total Time	1 h 25 m

Nutritional Information:

Calories	106 kcal
Fat	2.5 g
Carbohydrates	16.1g
Protein	5.6 g
Cholesterol	< 1 mg
Sodium	< 834 mg

* Percent Daily Values are based on a 2,000 calorie diet.

CREAMY LIME CURRY SOUP

Ingredients

- 1 butternut squash, halved and seeded
- 1 tbsp olive oil
- Salt and ground black pepper to taste
- 2 C. vegetable broth
- 1 tsp garlic powder
- 1 tsp onion powder
- 1 tsp curry powder
- 1/2 C. sour cream
- 1 tbsp lime juice
- 1 lime, zested

Directions

- Set your oven to 350 degrees F before doing anything else and line a baking sheet with a piece of the foil.
- Arrange the butternut squash onto the prepared baking sheet, cut-side up.
- Coat the cut sides of squash with the olive oil and season with the salt and pepper.
- Cook in the oven for about 45-60 minutes.
- Remove the squash from the oven and keep aside to cool for about 10 minutes.

- Scrape the flesh from the roasted butternut squash and transfer into a large pan with the broth, garlic powder, onion powder, curry powder, salt and pepper and bring to a simmer.
- Simmer for about 10 minutes.
- Remove from the heat and keep aside to cool slightly.
- In a blender, add the soup mixture in batches and pulse till smooth.
- In a bowl, add the sour cream, lime juice and lime zest and beat till well combined.
- Serve the soup hot with a topping of the lime cream.

Amount per serving 4

Timing Information:

Preparation	15 m
Cooking	55 m
Total Time	1 h 20 m

Nutritional Information:

Calories	229 kcal
Fat	10 g
Carbohydrates	35.3g
Protein	4.2 g
Cholesterol	13 mg
Sodium	353 mg

* Percent Daily Values are based on a 2,000 calorie diet.

Northern Ireland Inspire Leeks and Celery Curry Soup

Ingredients

- 2 tbsp butter
- 3 leeks (white and pale green parts only), thinly sliced
- 1 clove garlic, minced
- 1 (32 fluid oz.) container chicken stock
- 1 1/2 C. thinly sliced carrots
- 2 stalks celery, thinly sliced
- 1 tsp curry powder
- 1/2 tsp ground turmeric
- 1/2 tsp ground ginger
- 1/8 tsp ground black pepper
- 1 pinch red pepper flakes
- 1 1/2 (12 oz.) cans light coconut milk

Directions

- In a large pan, melt the butter on medium heat and sauté the leeks and garlic for about 5 minutes.
- Stir in the chicken stock, carrots, celery, curry powder, turmeric, ginger, black pepper and red peppers flakes and bring to a boil.

- Reduce the heat to medium-low and simmer, covered for about 30 minutes.
- Stir in the coconut milk and simmer for about 1-2 minutes.

Amount per serving 4

Timing Information:

Preparation	20 m
Cooking	40 m
Total Time	1 h

Nutritional Information:

Calories	257 kcal
Fat	18.9 g
Carbohydrates	18.9g
Protein	3.6 g
Cholesterol	16 mg
Sodium	798 mg

* Percent Daily Values are based on a 2,000 calorie diet.

40-MINUTE CURRY CARROT SOUP

Ingredients

- 2 tbsp olive oil
- 1 1/2 lb. peeled carrots, cut into 1-inch chunks
- 1 large onion, cut into large dice
- 1 tbsp butter
- 1 pinch sugar
- 3 large garlic cloves, thickly sliced
- 2 tbsp curry powder
- 3 C. chicken broth
- 1 1/2 C. half-and-half
- Salt and freshly ground pepper, to taste
- Garnish: chopped roasted pistachios

Directions

- In a large sauté pan, heat the oil on medium-high heat and sauté the carrots and onion for about 7-8 minutes.
- Reduce the heat to low and stir in the butter, sugar and garlic.
- Cook for about 10 minutes, stirring occasionally.
- Add the curry powder and sauté for about 30-60 seconds.
- Increase the heat to medium-high.
- Add the broth and bring to a boil.

- Reduce the heat to low and simmer, partially covered for about 10 minutes.
- With an immersion blender, blend till smooth.
- Stir in the half-and-half, salt and pepper and cook till heated completely.
- Serve with a garnishing of the roasted pistachios.

Amount per serving 8

Timing Information:

Preparation	10m
Cooking	30m
Total Time	40m

Nutritional Information:

Calories	158 kcal
Fat	10.9 g
Carbohydrates	13.5g
Protein	3.1 g
Cholesterol	34 mg
Sodium	101 mg

* Percent Daily Values are based on a 2,000 calorie diet.

Bangkok Lime Tomato and Shrimp Curry Soup

Ingredients

- 1/4 C. red curry paste, see appendix
- 2 tbsp olive oil
- 3 C. coconut milk
- 3 C. chicken stock
- 2 limes, juiced
- 1 lime, zested
- 2 C. cherry tomatoes
- 1 tbsp chopped fresh cilantro
- 1 lb. shrimp
- 1 (14 oz.) can bean sprouts, drained
- 1 C. chopped cooked chicken
- Salt and ground black pepper to taste

Directions

- In a pan, mix together the red curry paste and olive oil on low heat and sauté for about 5 minutes.
- Add the coconut milk, chicken stock, lime juice and lime zest and bring to a boil.

- Reduce the heat to medium-low and simmer for about 10 minutes.
- Stir in the cherry tomatoes and cilantro and again bring to a boil.
- Simmer for about 10-15 minutes.
- Stir in the shrimp, bean sprouts and cooked chicken and simmer for about 10-15 minutes.
- Stir in the salt and pepper and serve.

Amount per serving 8

Timing Information:

Preparation	10 m
Cooking	35 m
Total Time	45 m

Nutritional Information:

Calories	306 kcal
Fat	28.7 g
Carbohydrates	8.1g
Protein	19.2 g
Cholesterol	100 mg
Sodium	557 mg

* Percent Daily Values are based on a 2,000 calorie diet.

SATURDAY SUMMER PUMPKIN CURRY SOUP

Ingredients

- 1 (15 oz.) can pure pumpkin puree
- 2 C. Swanson(R) Chicken Broth
- 1/2 C. fat free half-and-half
- 1/2 tsp curry powder
- 1/8 tsp ground nutmeg
- Salt and freshly ground black pepper to taste
- 1/4 C. reduced-fat sour cream
- 1 tbsp chopped fresh chives

Directions

- In a medium pan, mix together the pumpkin puree and broth together on medium heat.
- Stir in the half-and-half, curry powder, nutmeg, salt, and pepper and cook for about 10 minutes.
- Serve with a garnishing of the sour cream and chopped chives.

Amount per serving 4

Timing Information:

Preparation	5 m
Cooking	10 m
Total Time	15 m

Nutritional Information:

Calories	81 kcal
Fat	2.9 g
Carbohydrates	12.7g
Protein	3 g
Cholesterol	10 mg
Sodium	1368 mg

* Percent Daily Values are based on a 2,000 calorie diet.

PERSIAN INSPIRED SAFFRON AND TOMATO CURRY SOUP

Ingredients

- 1 (14 oz.) can diced tomatoes, drained and juice reserved
- 1/4 C. extra virgin olive oil
- Salt and black pepper to taste
- 2 tbsp butter
- 2 large pinches saffron
- 1 stalk celery, diced
- 1 small carrot, diced
- 1 yellow onion, diced
- 2 cloves garlic, minced
- 1 C. chicken broth
- 1/2 tsp curry powder
- 1 tsp lime juice
- 2 tbsp chopped cilantro

Directions

- Set your oven to 350 degrees F before doing anything else.
- Spread the drained tomatoes onto a rimmed baking sheet.
- Drizzle with the olive oil and sprinkle with the salt and pepper.

- Cook in the oven for about 20 minutes.
- In a large pan, melt the butter on medium-low heat and sauté the saffron, celery, carrot, onion and garlic; for about 10 minutes.
- Stir in the roasted tomatoes, reserved tomato juices and chicken broth and simmer for about 15-20 minutes.
- Add the curry powder, lime juice and cilantro and stir to combine.
- With an immersion blender, blend the soup till smooth.
- Serve immediately.

Amount per serving 4

Timing Information:

Preparation	15 m
Cooking	45 m
Total Time	1 h

Nutritional Information:

Calories	222 kcal
Fat	19.9 g
Carbohydrates	8.8g
Protein	1.6 g
Cholesterol	15 mg
Sodium	217 mg

* Percent Daily Values are based on a 2,000 calorie diet.

OKANAGAN FRUITY MADRAS PEACH SOUP CURRY

Ingredients

- 5 tbsp olive oil
- 2 tbsp Madras curry powder
- 1 large onion, minced
- 3 cloves garlic, minced
- 1 (15 oz.) can sliced peaches in syrup, chopped
- 1 (14.5 oz.) can chopped plum tomatoes
- 1 tsp ground ginger
- 1 C. cream
- 1 C. vegetable broth
- Salt and black pepper to taste
- 2 C. lettuce, chopped
- 2 C. shelled, cooked shrimp

Directions

- In a large pan, heat the oil on medium heat and sauté the curry powder for about 1 minute.
- Add the onion and garlic and cook for about 8-10 minutes.

- Stir in the peaches with syrup, tomatoes, ginger, cream, broth, salt and pepper.
- Reduce the heat to low and simmer for about 45 minutes.
- Serve hot with a topping of the shrimp and lettuce.

Amount per serving 4

Timing Information:

Preparation	25 m
Cooking	45 m
Total Time	1 h 10 m

Nutritional Information:

Calories	523 kcal
Fat	40.4 g
Carbohydrates	26.3g
Protein	17.5 g
Cholesterol	206 mg
Sodium	437 mg

* Percent Daily Values are based on a 2,000 calorie diet.

PASTORAL MUSHROOM AND RICE CURRY SOUP

Ingredients

- 1 C. uncooked wild rice
- 1/4 C. butter
- 1 onion, chopped
- 2 1/2 C. sliced fresh mushrooms
- 1/2 C. chopped celery
- 1/2 C. all-purpose flour
- 6 C. vegetable broth
- 2 C. half-and-half
- 2/3 C. dry sherry
- 1/2 tsp salt
- 1/2 tsp white pepper
- 1/2 tsp curry powder
- 1/2 tsp dry mustard
- 1/2 tsp paprika
- 1/2 tsp dried chervil
- 1 tbsp chopped fresh parsley, for garnish

Directions

- In a pan of the boiling water, stir in the rice.

- Reduce the heat and simmer, covered for about 40 minutes.
- In a large pan, melt the butter on medium heat and sauté the onion till golden brown.
- Add the mushrooms and celery and sauté for about 2 minutes.
- Reduce the heat to low.
- Stir in the flour and cook till the mixture becomes bubbly, stirring continuously.
- Slowly, add the broth, stirring continuously.
- Increase the heat to medium-high and bring to a boil, stirring continuously.
- Reduce the heat to low and stir in the cooked rice, half and half, sherry, salt, white pepper, curry powder, dry mustard, paprika and chervil.
- Simmer till heated completely.
- Serve hot with a garnishing of the parsley.

Amount per serving 7

Timing Information:

Preparation	10 m
Cooking	45 m
Total Time	55 m

Nutritional Information:

Calories	176 kcal
Fat	9 g
Carbohydrates	19.2g
Protein	4.1 g
Cholesterol	25 mg
Sodium	456 mg

* Percent Daily Values are based on a 2,000 calorie diet.

AGRARIAN MUSTARD SEED CURRY SOUP

Ingredients

- 1 head cauliflower, cut into florets
- 2 tbsp olive oil
- 2 tsp curry powder
- 2 tsp mustard seeds
- 5 tbsp butter, divided
- 1/3 C. chopped sweet onion
- 6 C. chicken broth
- 3 tbsp all-purpose flour
- 1 C. milk
- Salt and ground black pepper to taste

Directions

- Set your oven to 350 degrees F before doing anything else.
- In a baking dish, add the cauliflower, olive oil, curry powder and mustard seeds and toss to coat.
- Cook in the oven for about 35-40 minutes.
- In a large pan, melt 2 tbsp of the butter on medium heat and sauté the onion for about 5-10 minutes.
- Add the chicken broth and cauliflower and bring to a boil.
- Reduce heat to low and simmer.

- Meanwhile for the roux in a small pan, mix together 3 tbsp of the butter and flour on medium-low heat.
- Cook for about 5 minutes, stirring continuously.
- Stir in the milk to roux and cook for about 5-10 minutes, stirring continuously.
- Add the roux into the soup and stir till smooth.
- Stir in the salt and pepper and serve.

Amount per serving 8

Timing Information:

Preparation	10 m
Cooking	50 m
Total Time	1 h

Nutritional Information:

Calories	157 kcal
Fat	12 g
Carbohydrates	9.5g
Protein	3.9 g
Cholesterol	25 mg
Sodium	825 mg

* Percent Daily Values are based on a 2,000 calorie diet.

SPINACH CREAM

Ingredients

- 1 1/2 C. water
- 3 cubes chicken bouillon
- 1 (10 oz) package frozen chopped spinach
- 3 tbsp butter
- 1/4 C. all-purpose flour
- 3 C. milk
- 1 tbsp dried minced onion
- Salt and pepper to taste

Directions

- Place a heavy saucepan over medium heat. Add the water, bouillon, and spinach then cook them until they start boiling.
- Place a saucepan over medium heat. Add the butter and melt it. Add the flour and mix them well while cooking them for 2 min.
- Drizzle the milk on them gradually while whisking all the time until they become smooth and cream.

- Add the minced onion, salt, and pepper then stir them for 5 min on low heat until they thicken. Stir in the spinach mix and simmer them for 2 min.
- Adjust the seasoning of the soup then serve it warm.
- Enjoy.

Amount per serving 4

Timing Information:

Preparation	5 m
Cooking	20 m
Total Time	25 m

Nutritional Information:

Calories	227 kcal
Fat	12.9 g
Carbohydrates	19.1g
Protein	10.1 g
Cholesterol	38 mg
Sodium	1053 mg

* Percent Daily Values are based on a 2,000 calorie diet.

POTATO FLAKES SOUP

Ingredients

- 6 slices bacon, diced
- 1 onion, chopped
- 1 tbsp all-purpose flour
- 6 C. chicken broth
- 6 potatoes, thinly sliced
- 1/2 C. instant mashed potato flakes
- 1 C. half-and-half

Directions

- Cook the bacon in a large skillet with onion for 6 min then drain then place them aside.
- Cook the flour for 1 min in a large saucepan then drizzle on it the broth while stirring all the time. Cook them until they start boiling.
- Add the cooked onion mix with the potatoes, a pinch of salt and pepper. Lower the heat and put on the lid then cook the soup for 35 min.
- Adjust the seasoning of the soup then serve it warm.
- Enjoy.

Amount per serving 8

Timing Information:

Preparation	15 m
Cooking	40 m
Total Time	55 m

Nutritional Information:

Calories	307 kcal
Fat	14.2 g
Carbohydrates	34.3g
Protein	10.7 g
Cholesterol	25 mg
Sodium	773 mg

* Percent Daily Values are based on a 2,000 calorie diet.

CHUNKY ASPARAGUS SOUP

Ingredients

- 3 slices bacon
- 1 tbsp bacon drippings
- 1/4 C. butter
- 3 stalks celery, chopped
- 1 onion, diced
- 3 tbsp all-purpose flour
- 6 C. chicken broth
- 1 potato, peeled and diced
- 1 lb fresh asparagus, tips set aside and stalks chopped
- Salt and ground black pepper to taste
- 1 (8 oz) package sliced fresh mushrooms
- 3/4 C. half-and-half cream

Directions

- Place a large pan over medium heat. Cook in it the bacon slices until they become crispy then drain them and place it aside to drain. Reserve 1 tbsp of bacon grease.
- Place a large saucepan over medium heat. Melt in the bacon grease with butter. Add the celery with onion and cook them for 5 min.

- Mix in the flour and cook them for 2 min. add the chicken broth gradually while stirring all the time. Cook the soup until it starts boiling.
- Stir in the asparagus stalks with potato, a pinch of salt and pepper. Lower the heat and put on the lid. Cook the soup for 22 min. allow the soup to cool down for 10 min.
- Get a food processor: Add the soup in batches and blend it smooth then pour it back into the pot.
- Cook the asparagus tips with mushroom, a pinch of salt and pepper in the pan where you cooked the bacon. Cook them for 7 min.
- Add the mushroom mix half and half to the soup and bring it to a boil. Crumble the bacon and serve it with the soup as a topping.
- Enjoy.

Amount per serving 8

Timing Information:

Preparation	15 m
Cooking	40 m
Total Time	55 m

Nutritional Information:

Calories	182 kcal
Fat	12.1 g
Carbohydrates	13.5g
Protein	5.9 g
Cholesterol	33 mg
Sodium	867 mg

* Percent Daily Values are based on a 2,000 calorie diet.

Chicken and Celery Cream Soup

Ingredients

- 3 quarts chicken stock
- 3 lb celery, coarsely chopped
- 1/2 lb carrots, julienned
- 1/2 lb onions, chopped
- 1 C. all-purpose flour
- 1 tbsp salt
- 1 tsp ground white pepper
- 3 quarts hot milk
- 1 C. margarine

Directions

- Place a large pot over medium heat. Add the stock and cook it until it starts boiling. Stir in the carrot with celery and onion.
- Get a small mixing bowl: Add the flour, salt, pepper, and milk. Mix them well. Stir the mix into the broth with margarine.
- Cook the soup until it starts boiling. Keep boiling the soup for 12 min. Drain the veggies and place them aside for

another use. Adjust the seasoning of the soup then serve it warm.

- Enjoy.

Amount per serving 32

Timing Information:

Preparation	20 m
Cooking	20 m
Total Time	40 m

Nutritional Information:

Calories	126 kcal
Fat	7.8 g
Carbohydrates	10.3g
Protein	4.1 g
Cholesterol	8 mg
Sodium	615 mg

* Percent Daily Values are based on a 2,000 calorie diet.

SWISS CAULIFLOWER SOUP

Ingredients

- 5 tbsp unsalted butter
- 1 leek, chopped
- 1 onion, chopped
- 1 carrot, chopped
- 1 tsp dried tarragon
- 1/2 tsp dried thyme
- 1/4 C. all-purpose flour
- 1 C. dry white wine
- 6 C. chicken stock
- Salt to taste
- 1/4 tsp freshly ground white pepper
- 1 head cauliflower, broken into small florets
- 1 C. milk
- 1 C. heavy whipping cream
- 2 1/2 C. shredded Swiss cheese (optional)

Directions

- Bring a salted pot of water to a boil. Place on it a steamer and cook in it the cauliflower until it becomes tender.

- Place a large pot over medium heat. Cook in the margarine until it melts. Add the leek, onion, and carrot then cook them for 12 min.
- Add the thyme with tarragon and cook them for 2 min. Stir in the flour for 1 min. Lower the heat and add the stock with wine, a pinch of salt and pepper.
- Stir in the cauliflower and bring the soup to a simmer. Remove the lid and cook the soup over low heat for 32 min.
- Get a food processor: Allow the soup to cool down for 10 min. blend the soup in batches in the food processor until it becomes smooth and creamy.
- Pour the soup back into the pot. Add the cream with milk and cook the soup for 5 min. Stir in the cheese until it melts.
- Adjust the seasoning of the soup then serve it warm.
- Enjoy.

Amount per serving 12

Timing Information:

Preparation	20 m
Cooking	20 m
Total Time	40 m

Nutritional Information:

Calories	256 kcal
Fat	18.9 g
Carbohydrates	10.3g
Protein	8.7 g
Cholesterol	62 mg
Sodium	81 mg

* Percent Daily Values are based on a 2,000 calorie diet.

CAULIFLOWER CREAM CURRY

Ingredients

- 1 head cauliflower, cut into florets
- 2 tbsp vegetable oil
- 1 tsp salt
- 1 tbsp butter, cut into small pieces
- 1 large yellow onion, diced
- 1 tsp chopped garlic
- 1 tsp curry powder
- 1 tsp cayenne pepper
- 1 tsp ground turmeric
- 1 quart chicken stock
- 1 C. heavy whipping cream
- Salt and ground black pepper to taste
- 2 tbsp chopped fresh parsley

Directions

- Before you do anything set the oven to 450 F.
- Combine the cauliflower florets with vegetable oil and 1 tsp in a large mixing bowl. Place the mix on a lined up baking pan.

- Cook the cauliflower in the oven for 28 min while stirring it every 10 min.
- Place a large saucepan over medium heat. Add the butter and cook it until it melts. Cook in it the onion for 6 min. add the garlic and cook them for 3 min.
- Stir in the curry powder, cayenne pepper, and ground turmeric. Cook them for 6 min while stirring them often.
- Add the stock with cooked cauliflower. Cook them until they start boiling. Remove the lid and lower the heat. Cook the soup for 12 min.
- Get a food processor: Allow the soup to cool down for 10 min. blend the soup in batches in the food processor until it becomes smooth and creamy.
- Pour the soup back into the pot. Add the cream with a pinch of salt and pepper then cook it for 5 min.
- Adjust the seasoning of the soup then serve it warm.
- Enjoy.

Amount per serving 4

Timing Information:

Preparation	15 m
Cooking	50 m
Total Time	1 h 5 m

Nutritional Information:

Calories	359 kcal
Fat	32.7 g
Carbohydrates	15.1g
Protein	5.4 g
Cholesterol	90 mg
Sodium	1391 mg

* Percent Daily Values are based on a 2,000 calorie diet.

HEALING SPRING SOUP

Ingredients

- 1 C. chopped green onions
- 1 C. chopped spinach
- 1/2 C. chopped fresh basil
- 1/2 C. chopped parsley
- 5 C. chicken broth
- 1 tsp white sugar
- 1 C. half-and-half cream
- Salt to taste
- Ground black pepper to taste
- 2 tbsp butter
- 2 tbsp all-purpose flour

Directions

- Place a large pot over medium heat. Add 3 tbsp of butter and cook it until it melts. Add the onion and cook it for 12 min.
- Stir in the spinach, basil or watercress, and parsley. Lower the heat and put on the lid. Cook the soup for 12 min.
- Add the sugar with broth. Put on the lid and cook the soup for 32 min. add the cream gradually while stirring the soup all the time.

- Place a small saucepan over medium heat. Cook in it 2 tbsp of butter until it melts. Add the flour and cook it for 2 min while mixing all the time.
- Add some of the hot soup to the pan and stir it until the mix becomes smooth. Transfer the mix to the soup and stir it until it starts boiling.
- Adjust the seasoning of the soup then serve it warm.
- Enjoy.

Amount per serving 8

Timing Information:

Preparation	15 m
Cooking	45 m
Total Time	1 h

Nutritional Information:

Calories	127 kcal
Fat	9.8 g
Carbohydrates	5.3g
Protein	4.7 g
Cholesterol	25 mg
Sodium	680 mg

* Percent Daily Values are based on a 2,000 calorie diet.

CHICKEN FLAVORED BROCCOLI SOUP

Ingredients

- 3 tbsp butter
- 1 onion, chopped
- 4 large carrots, chopped
- 1 clove garlic, chopped
- 4 C. water
- 4 tbsp chicken bouillon powder
- 1 lb fresh broccoli florets
- 2 C. half-and-half
- 3 tbsp all-purpose flour
- 1/4 C. ice water
- 1 tbsp soy sauce
- 1/2 tsp ground black pepper
- 1/4 C. chopped parsley

Directions

- Place a large saucepan over medium heat. Cook in it the butter until it melts. Stir in the onions, carrots, and garlic. Cook them for 6 in. Reserve 1/2 C. of broccoli florets.

- Combine 4 C. water and chicken bouillon granules in a large pot. Cook them until they start boiling. Add the cooked onion mix with broccoli florets.
- Lower the heat and put on the lid. Cook the soup for 18 min.
- Get a food processor: Allow the soup to cool down for 10 min. blend the soup in batches in the food processor with the remaining broccoli and half and half cream until it becomes smooth and creamy.
- Pour the soup back into the pot. Cook the soup until it starts boiling. Mix 1/4 C. of water with flour in a small bowl. Stir it into the soup while boiling and cook it until it thickens.
- Stir in the soy sauce with a pinch of salt and pepper. Adjust the seasoning of the soup then serve it warm.
- Enjoy.

Amount per serving 6

Timing Information:

Preparation	20 m
Cooking	45 m
Total Time	1 h 5 m

Nutritional Information:

Calories	247 kcal
Fat	16.3 g
Carbohydrates	20.2g
Protein	7.5 g
Cholesterol	48 mg
Sodium	1721 mg

* Percent Daily Values are based on a 2,000 calorie diet.

Chilled Summer Mango Soup

Ingredients

- 2 mango - peeled, seeded, and cubed
- 1/4 C. white sugar
- 1 lemon, zested and juiced
- 1 1/2 C. half-and-half

Directions

- Get a blender: Combine all the
- Ingredients in it and blend them smooth.
- Chill the soup in the fridge until ready to serve.
- Enjoy.

Amount per serving 3

Timing Information:

Preparation	10 m
Total Time	10 m

Nutritional Information:

Calories	319 kcal
Fat	14.4 g
Carbohydrates	49.2g
Protein	4.7 g
Cholesterol	45 mg
Sodium	53 mg

* Percent Daily Values are based on a 2,000 calorie diet.

Italian Basil Tomato Soup

Ingredients

- 1 (26 oz) can tomato soup
- 2 (14.5 oz) cans Italian-style diced tomatoes, undrained
- 1/2 C. water
- 1 C. milk
- 4 oz crumbled Gorgonzola cheese
- 2 tbsp minced garlic
- 1 tbsp dried basil
- 1 tsp onion powder

Directions

- Place a large saucepan over medium heat. Stir in all the
- Ingredients put on the lid and lower the heat. Cook the soup for 18 min.
- Adjust the seasoning of the soup then serve it warm.
- Enjoy.

Amount per serving 4

Timing Information:

Preparation	10 m
Cooking	15 m
Total Time	25 m

Nutritional Information:

Calories	251 kcal
Fat	9.6 g
Carbohydrates	26.1g
Protein	11.6 g
Cholesterol	38 mg
Sodium	1148 mg

* Percent Daily Values are based on a 2,000 calorie diet.

FANCY VERMOUTH ARTICHOKE SOUP

Ingredients

- 4 whole artichokes
- 2 C. water
- 2 C. chicken stock
- 1/2 C. dry vermouth, optional
- 1 potato, diced
- 1 small carrot, diced
- 1 onion, chopped
- 1 small stalk celery, diced
- 2 cloves garlic, minced
- 2 bay leaves
- 1/2 tsp dried marjoram
- 1 C. heavy whipping cream
- 4 tbsp grated Romano cheese
- Salt to taste
- Ground black pepper to taste

Directions

- Bring 2 C. of water in a large saucepan and bring it to a boil. Place a steamer on it and cook in it the artichokes for 46 min.

- Place the artichokes aside to lose heat. Reserve the cooking water of the artichokes. Cut the artichoke hearts into dices.
- Place a large pot over medium heat. Stir in the artichoke heart dices with chicken stock, vermouth, potato, carrot, onion, celery, garlic, bay leaves, and marjoram.
- Lower the heat and cook the soup for 47 min.
- Get a food processor: Allow the soup to cool down for 10 min. blend the soup in batches in the food processor until it becomes smooth and creamy.
- Pour the soup back into the pot with cheese and cream. Adjust the seasoning of the soup then serve it warm.
- Enjoy.

Amount per serving 4

Timing Information:

Preparation	10 m
Cooking	15 m
Total Time	25 m

Nutritional Information:

Calories	410 kcal
Fat	24.6 g
Carbohydrates	33.8g
Protein	10 g
Cholesterol	92 mg
Sodium	735 mg

* Percent Daily Values are based on a 2,000 calorie diet.

BELL CHEESE SOUP

Ingredients

- 1/4 C. butter
- 1 small onion, minced
- 3 stalks celery, chopped
- 1/4 C. all-purpose flour
- 4 C. chicken stock
- 1/2 lb Brie cheese with the rind, cubed
- 1/2 C. heavy cream
- 1 tbsp green bell pepper, cut into very fine matchsticks
- 1 tbsp red bell pepper, cut into very fine matchsticks

Directions

- Place a large saucepan over medium heat. Add the butter and cook it until it melts. Sauté in it the celery with onion for 6 min
- Add the flour and cook them for 4 min. Add the stock gradually while mixing them gently all the time. Lower the heat and cook the soup for 22 min.
- Add the brie cheese and stir it gently until it melts for 6 min.

- Get a food processor: Allow the soup to cool down for 10 min. blend the soup in batches in the food processor until it becomes smooth and creamy.
- Pour the soup back into the pot. Cook the soup until it starts simmering. Stir in the cream. Adjust the seasoning of the soup then serve it warm.
- Enjoy.

Amount per serving 4

Timing Information:

Preparation	25 m
Cooking	30 m
Total Time	55 m

Nutritional Information:

Calories	395 kcal
Fat	33.5 g
Carbohydrates	10.5g
Protein	14.1 g
Cholesterol	108 mg
Sodium	1155 mg

* Percent Daily Values are based on a 2,000 calorie diet.

TAIWANESE CORN SOUP

Ingredients

- 1 (15 oz.) can cream style corn
- 1 (14.5 oz.) can low-sodium chicken broth
- 1 egg, beaten
- 1 tbsp cornstarch
- 2 tbsps water

Directions

- Get the following boiling in a large pot: broth and cream corn.
- Get a bowl, combine: water and cornstarch.
- Mix the contents until smooth then add the mix with the boiling broth.
- Let the broth continue to cook for 4 mins then add the whisked eggs slowly.
- Stir the soup while adding in your eggs.
- Enjoy.

Amount per serving: (4 total)

Timing Information:

Preparation	5 m
Cooking	10 m
Total Time	15 m

Nutritional Information:

Calories	121 kcal
Fat	1.9 g
Carbohydrates	24.1g
Protein	5 g
Cholesterol	48 mg
Sodium	409 mg

* Percent Daily Values are based on a 2,000 calorie diet.

Easy Egg and Pea Soup

Ingredients

- 4 C. seasoned chicken broth
- 1/2 C. frozen green peas
- 1 egg, beaten

Directions

- Get your peas and broth boiling. Then once the mix is boiling add in your whisked eggs gradually to form ribbons.
- Then add in your green onions and serve.
- Enjoy.

Amount per serving: (6 total)

Timing Information:

Preparation	2 m
Cooking	13 m
Total Time	15 m

Nutritional Information:

Calories	35 kcal
Fat	1.9 g
Carbohydrates	2.5g
Protein	< 2.4 g
Cholesterol	31 mg
Sodium	639 mg

* Percent Daily Values are based on a 2,000 calorie diet.

ASIAN CORN SOUP CREAM STYLE

Ingredients

- 1/2 lb skinless, boneless chicken breast meat - finely diced
- 1 tbsp sherry
- 1/4 tsp salt
- 2 egg whites
- 1 (14.75 oz.) can cream-style corn
- 4 C. chicken broth
- 2 tsps soy sauce
- 1/4 C. water
- 2 tbsps cornstarch
- 4 slices crisp cooked bacon, crumbled

Directions

- Get a bowl, combine: chicken, egg whites, sherry, and salt.
- Combine in the cream corn and continue mixing everything until it's smooth.
- Now get the following boiling in a wok: soy sauce and chicken broth.
- Combine in the chicken mix and get everything boiling again.

- Now set the heat to low, and cook the soup for 5 mins while stirring.
- Combine some cornstarch and water then pour this mix into your boiling soup and keep stirring everything for 3 more mins. Then add in your bacon and serve.
- Enjoy.

Amount per serving: (6 total)

Timing Information:

Preparation	10 m
Cooking	30 m
Total Time	50 m

Nutritional Information:

Calories	157 kcal
Fat	3.3 g
Carbohydrates	16.2g
Protein	16 g
Cholesterol	26 mg
Sodium	1052 mg

* Percent Daily Values are based on a 2,000 calorie diet.

BAMBOO RICE SOUP

Ingredients

- 3 oz. baby shrimp
- 3 oz. skinless, boneless chicken pieces cut into chunks
- 1 egg
- 4 tbsps cornstarch
- 4 C. vegetable oil for frying
- 3 C. chicken broth
- 1 oz. mushrooms, diced
- 2 tbsps diced water chestnuts
- 1/8 C. diced bamboo shoots
- 1/3 C. fresh green beans, cut into 1 inch pieces
- 1/2 tsp salt
- 1 tbsp sherry, optional
- 2/3 C. uncooked white rice

Directions

- Get a bowl, combine: cornstarch, shrimp, egg, and chicken.
- Get 3 C. of oil hot in a frying pan then add the chicken mix.
- Fry the mix for 1 min then remove the oils.

- Now add everything to a large pot with: the green beans, broth, bamboo shoots, salt, mushrooms, sherry, and water chestnuts.
- Get everything boiling, set the heat to low, and let the mix gently cook.
- At the time same as the soup is simmering get 1 C. of oil hot and toast your rice in it until the kernels are browned.
- Combine the rice with the soup and let the mix cook until the rice is tender.
- Enjoy.

Amount per serving: (6 total)

Timing Information:

Preparation	10 m
Cooking	15 m
Total Time	25 m

Nutritional Information:

Calories	295 kcal
Fat	17 g
Carbohydrates	24g
Protein	10.6 g
Cholesterol	60 mg
Sodium	641 mg

* Percent Daily Values are based on a 2,000 calorie diet.

POTATO SOUP

Ingredients

- 3 potatoes, cubed
- 1 carrot, diced
- 1 turnip, diced
- 1 onion, diced
- 5 cloves garlic, minced
- 1 chicken leg
- salt and pepper to taste

Directions

- Get the following boiling: water, potatoes, chicken, carrots, garlic, turnips, and onions.
- Once the mix is boiling, set the heat to a low level.
- Cook the mix for 50 mins then add some pepper and salt.
- Take out the chicken legs and remove their meat, once the chicken is cool enough to handle.

- Place the meat back into the soup. Throw away the bones and skin.
- Continue cooking the soup for 35 more mins.
- Enjoy.

Amount per serving: (3 total)

Timing Information:

Preparation	10 m
Cooking	1 h 45 m
Total Time	1 h 55 m

Nutritional Information:

Calories	255 kcal
Fat	2.8 g
Carbohydrates	47.2g
Protein	11.6 g
Cholesterol	19 mg
Sodium	77 mg

* Percent Daily Values are based on a 2,000 calorie diet.

SUAN LA DOFU TANG

(TOFU SOUP)

Ingredients

- 4 C. vegetable broth
- 1 (12 oz.) package silken tofu, diced
- 2 green onions, diced
- 1 eggs, beaten
- 1 portobello mushroom, halved and sliced
- 2 C. diced cabbage
- 1 tbsp Thai chile sauce
- 1 tbsp rice vinegar
- 3 tbsps soy sauce
- 1 tsp citric acid powder (optional)

Directions

- Get your broth boiling then add the green onions and tofu.
- Gradually pour in the whisked eggs to form long ribbons. Then combine in the cabbage and mushrooms.
- Let the contents cook for 7 mins then shut the heat.
- Add in your soy sauce, citric acid, vinegar, and chili sauce.

- Enjoy.

Amount per serving: (2 total)

Timing Information:

Preparation	15 m
Cooking	10 m
Total Time	25 m

Nutritional Information:

Calories	256 kcal
Fat	8.3 g
Carbohydrates	25.5g
Protein	21.2 g
Cholesterol	93 mg
Sodium	2390 mg

* Percent Daily Values are based on a 2,000 calorie diet.

Hot and Spicy Soup

Ingredients

- 5 dried wood ear mushrooms
- 4 dried shiitake mushrooms
- 8 dried tiger lily buds
- 4 C. chicken stock
- 1/3 C. diced bamboo shoots
- 1/3 C. lean ground pork
- 1 tsp soy sauce
- 1/2 tsp white sugar
- 1 tsp salt
- 1/2 tsp ground white pepper
- 2 tbsps red wine vinegar
- 2 tbsps cornstarch
- 3 tbsps water
- 1/2 (16 oz.) package firm tofu, cubed
- 1 egg, lightly beaten
- 1 tsp sesame oil
- 2 tbsps thinly sliced green onion

Directions

- In warm water, for 30 mins, submerge your tiger lily and mushrooms, in a bowl.
- Now remove any stems and cut the mushrooms and tiger lilly.
- Now get the following boiling in a large pot: pork, mushrooms, bamboo shoots, tiger lily, and stock.
- Let the mix cook for 12 mins then add: vinegar, soy sauce, white pepper, sugar, and salt.
- Grab a small bowl, combine: some of the hot soup, 3 tbsps water, and cornstarch.
- Mix everything until it's smooth then combine everything together and stir.
- Get the mix completely boiling then add in the bean curds and cook the soup for 3 more mins.
- Now shut the heat and slowly add in the eggs.
- Let the eggs set then add the sesame oil and the scallions.
- Enjoy.

Amount per serving: (6 total)

Timing Information:

Preparation	30 m
Cooking	30 m
Total Time	1 h

Nutritional Information:

Calories	116 kcal
Fat	6.3 g
Carbohydrates	8.7g
Protein	7.4 g
Cholesterol	41 mg
Sodium	465 mg

* Percent Daily Values are based on a 2,000 calorie diet.

CHI TAN T'ANG

(CLASSICAL EGG DROP SOUP)

Ingredients

- 8 cubes chicken bouillon
- 6 C. hot water
- 2 tbsps cornstarch
- 2 tbsps soy sauce
- 3 tbsps distilled white vinegar
- 1 green onion, minced
- 3 eggs, beaten

Directions

- Get a large pot and begin to heat some hot water and bouillon.
- Stir and heat the mix until the bouillon is completely dissolved.
- Now add in: the green onions, soy sauce, and vinegar.
- Get the mix boiling then set the heat to low.
- Slowly add in your whisked eggs while stirring.
- Once the eggs have set, shut the heat.
- Enjoy.

Amount per serving: (6 total)

Timing Information:

Preparation	10 m
Cooking	10 m
Total Time	20 m

Nutritional Information:

Calories	62 kcal
Fat	2.8 g
Carbohydrates	4.7g
Protein	4.5 g
Cholesterol	94 mg
Sodium	1872 mg

* Percent Daily Values are based on a 2,000 calorie diet.

CABBAGE SOUP

Ingredients

- 1 1/2 tbsps vegetable oil
- 1/4 small head cabbage, shredded
- 4 oz. lean pork tenderloin, cut into thin strips
- 6 C. chicken broth
- 2 tbsps soy sauce
- 1/2 tsp minced fresh ginger root
- 8 fresh green onions, diced
- 4 oz. dry Chinese noodles

Directions

- Stir fry your pork and cabbage for 7 mins until the pork is fully done.
- Pour in the broth and add: ginger and soy sauce.
- Stir the mix then get everything boiling.
- Once the mix is boiling set the heat to low and let the mix cook for 12 mins.
- Stir the contents at least 3 times.
- Now add the noodles and onions and cook everything for 5 more mins.
- Enjoy.

Amount per serving: (4 total)

Timing Information:

Preparation	10 m
Cooking	30 m
Total Time	50 m

Nutritional Information:

Calories	256 kcal
Fat	8.9 g
Carbohydrates	28g
Protein	17.9 g
Cholesterol	18 mg
Sodium	1623 mg

* Percent Daily Values are based on a 2,000 calorie diet.

SWEET AND SPICY TOFU SOUP

Ingredients

- 1 tbsp vegetable oil
- 1 red bell pepper, diced
- 3 green onions, diced
- 2 C. water
- 2 C. chicken broth
- 1 tbsp soy sauce
- 1 tbsp red wine vinegar
- 1/4 tsp crushed red pepper flakes
- 1/8 tsp ground black pepper
- 1 tbsp cornstarch
- 3 tbsps water
- 1 tbsp sesame oil
- 6 oz. frozen snow peas
- 1 (8 oz.) package firm tofu, cubed
- 1 (8 oz.) can sliced water chestnuts, drained

Directions

- Stir fry your green onions and bell peppers in oil for 7 mins then combine in: soy sauce, broth, and 2 C. of water.

- Now set the heat to medium and let the mix cook for 7 more mins.
- Get a bowl, combine: sesame oil, vinegar, 3 tbsps water, pepper flakes, cornstarch, and black pepper.
- Stir the mix until it is smooth then pour it into the simmering broth.
- Continue simmering the broth for 7 more mins until it gets thick then add in: water chestnuts, snow peas, and tofu.
- Let the tofu cook for 12 mins.
- Enjoy.

Amount per serving: (4 total)

Timing Information:

Preparation	20 m
Cooking	30 m
Total Time	50 m

Nutritional Information:

Calories	211 kcal
Fat	12 g
Carbohydrates	17.3g
Protein	11.3 g
Cholesterol	0 mg
Sodium	243 mg

* Percent Daily Values are based on a 2,000 calorie diet.

EASY WONTON SOUP

Ingredients

- 8 C. chicken broth
- 3 tbsps soy sauce
- 2 tsps sesame oil
- 2 tsps rice wine vinegar
- 2 tsps lemon juice
- 2 tsps minced garlic
- 1 1/2 tsps chile-garlic sauce (such as Sriracha(R))
- salt to taste
- 8 C. water
- 20 wontons

Directions

- Get the following simmering: salt, broth, chili garlic sauce, sesame oil, garlic, wine vinegar, and lemon juice.
- Let the mix gently simmer for 12 mins.
- At the same time being to get some water boiling in another pot. Add the wontons to the boiling water and let the mix cook for 7 mins. Then combine the wontons to the simmering mix.
- Enjoy.

Amount per serving: (4 total)

Timing Information:

Preparation	5 m
Cooking	10 m
Total Time	15 m

Nutritional Information:

Calories	293 kcal
Fat	9 g
Carbohydrates	33.5g
Protein	17.7 g
Cholesterol	84 mg
Sodium	3373 mg

* Percent Daily Values are based on a 2,000 calorie diet.

ALTERNATIVE EGG DROP SOUP

Ingredients

- 1 egg
- 1/4 tsp salt
- 2 tbsps tapioca flour
- 1/4 C. cold water
- 4 C. chicken broth
- 1/8 tsp ground ginger
- 1/8 tsp minced fresh garlic
- 2 tbsps diced green onion
- 1/4 tsp Asian (toasted) sesame oil (optional)
- 1 pinch white pepper (optional)

Directions

- Get a bowl and whisk your eggs with salt in it.
- Get a 2nd bowl, mix: cold water and tapioca flour. Mix everything until its smooth.
- Now get your garlic, ginger, and broth boiling.
- Once the mix has boiled for about 2 mins add the tapioca mix and continue boiling everything for about 2 more mins until the mix is no longer cloudy and thick.

- Remove the mix from the heat and add the eggs in gradually.
- Combine the eggs in slowly in the form of a circle but do not stir the mix too much.
- Once the eggs have set add a garnishing of white pepper, sesame oil, and onions.
- Enjoy.

Amount per serving: (4 total)

Timing Information:

Preparation	10 m
Cooking	10 m
Total Time	20 m

Nutritional Information:

Calories	36 kcal
Fat	1.6 g
Carbohydrates	4g
Protein	1.7 g
Cholesterol	46 mg
Sodium	164 mg

* Percent Daily Values are based on a 2,000 calorie diet.

SLIGHTLY SPICY POTATO SOUP

Ingredients

- 2 tbsp butter
- 1 C. diced onion
- 2 1/2 C. peeled and diced potatoes
- 3 C. chicken broth
- 1 C. heavy cream
- 1 3/4 C. shredded sharp Cheddar cheese
- 1/4 tsp dried dill weed
- 1/4 tsp ground black pepper
- 1/4 tsp salt
- 1/8 tsp ground cayenne pepper

Directions

- In a large pan, melt the butter on medium heat and cook the onion till softened.
- Stir in the potatoes and broth and bring to a boil.
- Reduce the heat and simmer, covered for about 15-20 minutes.
- With an immersion blender, puree the potato mixture.
- Place the pan on medium heat and stir in the cream, cheese, dill, pepper, salt and cayenne.

- Bring to a low boil and cook, stirring continuously for about 5 minutes.

Amount per serving (6 total)

Timing Information:

Preparation	15 m
Cooking	30 m
Total Time	45 m

Nutritional Information:

Calories	366 kcal
Fat	29.6 g
Carbohydrates	16g
Protein	10.4 g
Cholesterol	99 mg
Sodium	348 mg

* Percent Daily Values are based on a 2,000 calorie diet.

SIMPLE YUKON POTATO SOUP

Ingredients

- 1 C. butter
- 2 leeks, sliced
- salt and pepper to taste
- 1 quart chicken broth
- 1 tbsp cornstarch
- 4 C. Yukon Gold potatoes, peeled and diced
- 2 C. heavy cream

Directions

- In a large pan, melt the butter on medium heat and sauté the leeks for about 15 minutes.
- In a bowl, mix together the cornstarch and broth.
- In the pan, add the potatoes and broth mixture and bring to a boil.
- Season with the salt and pepper.
- Stir in the cream and reduce the heat.
- Simmer for about 30 minutes.
- Season with the salt and pepper before serving.

Amount per serving (8 total)

Timing Information:

Preparation	15 m
Cooking	1 h
Total Time	1 h 15 m

Nutritional Information:

Calories	488 kcal
Fat	45.4 g
Carbohydrates	18.7g
Protein	3.7 g
Cholesterol	145 mg
Sodium	673 mg

* Percent Daily Values are based on a 2,000 calorie diet.

ALL YOU NEED IS THYME POTATO SOUP

Ingredients

- 1/4 C. butter
- 1 large onion, chopped
- 6 potatoes, peeled and diced
- 2 carrots, diced
- 3 C. water
- 2 tbsp chicken bouillon powder
- ground black pepper to taste
- 3 tbsp all-purpose flour
- 3 C. milk
- 1 tbsp dried parsley
- 1/4 tsp dried thyme

Directions

- In a pan, melt the butter on medium heat and sauté the onion for about 5 minutes.
- Meanwhile in another pan, add the potatoes, carrots, water and chicken soup base and bring to a boil.
- Cook for about 10 minutes.
- Season with the ground black pepper to taste.
- Add the flour, stirring continuously till smooth.

- Cook, stirring continuously for about 2 minutes.
- Slowly, add the milk and stir well.
- Reduce the heat to low heat and cook, stirring continuously till warmed completely.
- Add the potato and carrot mixture, parsley and thyme and cook till heated completely.
- Serve hot.

Amount per serving (6 total)

Timing Information:

Preparation	20 m
Cooking	25 m
Total Time	45 m

Nutritional Information:

Calories	338 kcal
Fat	10.8 g
Carbohydrates	51.6g
Protein	10.1 g
Cholesterol	31 mg
Sodium	857 mg

* Percent Daily Values are based on a 2,000 calorie diet.

Swiss Style Potato Soup

Ingredients

- 4 potatoes, peeled and quartered
- 1 small carrot, finely chopped
- 1/2 stalk celery, finely chopped
- 1 small onion, minced
- 1 1/2 C. vegetable broth
- 1 tsp salt
- 2 1/2 C. milk
- 3 tbsp butter, melted
- 3 tbsp all-purpose flour
- 1 tbsp dried parsley
- 1 tsp ground black pepper
- 1 C. shredded Swiss cheese

Directions

- In a large pan, add the potatoes, carrots, celery, onion, vegetable broth and salt and bring to a boil.
- Reduce the heat and simmer, covered till the potatoes become just tender.
- With a potato masher, mash the mixture slightly and stir in the milk.

- In a small bowl, add the butter, flour, parsley and pepper and beat to combine.
- Add the butter mixture into the potato mixture.
- Cook and stir on the medium heat till the mixture becomes thick and bubbly.
- Remove from the heat and immediately, stir in the cheese and stir till the cheese is almost melted.
- Keep aside the soup for about 5 minutes.

Amount per serving (6 total)

Timing Information:

Preparation	30 m
Cooking	20 m
Total Time	50 m

Nutritional Information:

Calories	311 kcal
Fat	13.1 g
Carbohydrates	37.1g
Protein	12.1 g
Cholesterol	40 mg
Sodium	638 mg

* Percent Daily Values are based on a 2,000 calorie diet.

POTATO SOUP SUMMERS

Ingredients

- 12 potatoes, peeled and cubed
- 2 large onions, finely chopped
- 2 lb. processed cheese food
- 1 lb. chopped ham, optional
- ground black pepper to taste
- 3 1/2 tbsp all-purpose flour
- 1 C. milk

Directions

- In a large soup pan, mix together the potatoes, onion, and cubed ham.
- Add enough water and cook till the potatoes becomes almost tender.
- In a bowl, add about 1 C. of the cooked potatoes and with a fork, mash them.
- Add some of the liquid from the pan and in a bowl with the flour and mix till a thick paste form.
- Add the flour paste in the soup and stir to combine.
- Place the cubed cheese in the pan and simmer till the cheese melts completely.
- Add ground black pepper to taste and stir in the milk.

Amount per serving (16 total)

Timing Information:

Preparation	30 m
Cooking	40 m
Total Time	1 h 10 m

Nutritional Information:

Calories	321 kcal
Fat	9.4 g
Carbohydrates	39.6g
Protein	19.9 g
Cholesterol	42 mg
Sodium	1294 mg

* Percent Daily Values are based on a 2,000 calorie diet.

PEANUT POTATO SOUP

Ingredients

- 1/2 C. sour cream
- 1 tsp grated lime zest
- 2 large sweet potatoes, peeled and cubed
- 1 tbsp butter
- 1 onion, sliced
- 2 cloves garlic, sliced
- 4 C. chicken stock
- 1/2 tsp ground cumin
- 1/4 tsp crushed red pepper flakes
- 2 tbsp grated fresh ginger root
- 1/4 C. smooth peanut butter
- 1 lime, juiced
- 2 tbsp chopped fresh cilantro
- salt to taste
- 1 large roma (plum) tomato, seeded and diced

Directions

- In a small bowl, mix together the sour cream and lime zest and refrigerate to allow the flavors to blend.

- In a large pan, melt the butter on medium heat and sauté the onion and garlic for about 5 minutes.
- Add the sweet potatoes, chicken broth, cumin, chili flakes and ginger and bring to a boil.
- Reduce the heat to low, and simmer, covered for about 15 minutes.
- With an immersion blender, puree the soup.
- Add the peanut butter into the soup, beating continuously till well combined.
- Simmer till heated completely.
- Stir in the lime juice and salt.
- Place the soup into the warm bowls and top with a dollop of the reserved sour cream, a few pieces of the diced tomato and a sprinkle of the cilantro.

Amount per serving (8 total)

Timing Information:

Preparation	30 m
Cooking	20 m
Total Time	50 m

Nutritional Information:

Calories	207 kcal
Fat	9 g
Carbohydrates	28.7g
Protein	5 g
Cholesterol	11 mg
Sodium	462 mg

* Percent Daily Values are based on a 2,000 calorie diet.

Cream of Chicken Potato Soup

Ingredients

- 8 slices bacon, optional
- 1 C. chopped onion
- 4 C. cubed potatoes
- 2 (10.75 oz.) cans condensed cream of chicken soup
- 2 1/2 C. milk
- salt to taste
- ground black pepper to taste
- 1 tsp dried dill weed

Directions

- Heat a large pan and cook the bacon till browned completely.
- Transfer the bacon onto a paper towel lined plate to drain and then crumble it.
- Discard the bacon grease, leaving about 3 tbsp inside the pan.
- Heat the bacon grease on medium heat and cook the onion till browned.
- Add the potatoes and enough water to cover.
- Cook, covered for about 15-20 minutes.

- In a bowl, add the cream of chicken soup and milk and mix till smooth.
- Add the milk mixture into the soup mixture and cool till just heated.
- Stir in the salt, pepper and dill weed and remove from the heat.
- Serve the soup with a topping of the bacon.

Amount per serving (6 total)

Timing Information:

Preparation	10 m
Cooking	40 m
Total Time	50 m

Nutritional Information:

Calories	404 kcal
Fat	24.8 g
Carbohydrates	32.9g
Protein	12.5 g
Cholesterol	42 mg
Sodium	1026 mg

* Percent Daily Values are based on a 2,000 calorie diet.

CREAM OF MUSHROOM POTATO SOUP

Ingredients

- 8 unpeeled potatoes, cubed
- 1 onion, chopped
- 2 stalks celery, diced
- 6 cubes chicken bouillon
- 1 pint half-and-half cream
- 1 lb. bacon - cooked and crumbled, optional
- 1 (10.75 oz.) can condensed cream of mushroom soup
- 2 C. shredded Cheddar cheese

Directions

- In a large soup pan mix together the potatoes, onions, celery, bouillon cubes and enough water to cover the all ingredients and bring to a boil on medium heat.
- Simmer for about 15 minutes.
- Add the half and half, bacon and cream of mushroom soup and stir till smooth and creamy.
- Add the cheese and stir till melts completely.
- Simmer on low heat till the potatoes are cooked through.

Amount per serving (9 total)

Timing Information:

Preparation	30 m
Cooking	20 m
Total Time	50 m

Nutritional Information:

Calories	642 kcal
Fat	38.9 g
Carbohydrates	41.2g
Protein	31.8 g
Cholesterol	105 mg
Sodium	2352 mg

* Percent Daily Values are based on a 2,000 calorie diet.

PERFECT AUTUMN SOUP

Ingredients

- 2 tbsp butter
- 1 onion, diced
- 1/2 tsp ground cardamom
- 1/4 tsp ground turmeric
- 1/4 tsp ground ginger
- 1/4 tsp red pepper flakes
- 1/4 tsp ground cinnamon
- 1 pinch cayenne pepper
- 1 (14 oz.) can chicken broth
- 2 C. water
- 2 large sweet potatoes, peeled and diced
- 3 carrots, peeled and chopped
- Salt and pepper to taste

Directions

- In a large pan, melt the butter on medium-high heat and sauté the onion for about 5-7 minutes.
- Stir in the cardamom, turmeric, ginger, pepper flakes, cinnamon and cayenne and sauté for about 1 minute.

- Add the chicken broth, water, sweet potatoes and carrots and bring to a boil on high heat.
- Reduce the heat to medium-low and simmer, covered for about 25-30 minutes.
- Remove from the heat and keep aside to cool slightly.
- In a blender, add the soup in batches and pulse till smooth.

Amount per serving (4 total)

Timing Information:

Preparation	35 m
Cooking	30 m
Total Time	1 h 5 m

Nutritional Information:

Calories	286 kcal
Fat	6.3 g
Carbohydrates	53.7g
Protein	4.9 g
Cholesterol	18 mg
Sodium	765 mg

* Percent Daily Values are based on a 2,000 calorie diet.

Anti-Inflammatory Potato Soup

Ingredients

- 6 oz. egg noodles
- 3 tbsp extra-virgin olive oil
- 1 (2 inch) piece ginger root, minced
- 2 cloves garlic, minced
- 1 leek, sliced into 1/2-inch pieces
- 2 carrots, cut into cubes
- 2 stalks celery, sliced into 1/2-inch pieces
- 2 potatoes, peeled and cubed
- 1 tsp turmeric powder
- 1/2 tsp ground white pepper
- 1/2 tsp salt
- 3 C. water
- 2 C. vegetable broth

Directions

- In large pan of the lightly salted boiling water, cook the egg noodles for about 3 minutes.
- Drain well.
- In a large pan, heat the oil on medium heat and sauté the garlic and ginger for about 1 minute.

- Stir in the leeks and cook for about 3 minutes.
- Stir in the carrots and celery and cook for about 2 minutes.
- Stir in the potatoes and cook for about 2 minutes.
- Cook, covered for about 5 minutes.
- Stir in the turmeric, white pepper, salt and water and bring to a boil.
- In another pan, add the vegetable broth and bring to a boil.
- Remove from the heat and stir in the potato soup mixture.
- Stir in the egg noodles and simmer for about 5 minutes.

Amount per serving (4 total)

Timing Information:

Preparation	30 m
Cooking	31 m
Total Time	1 h 2 m

Nutritional Information:

Calories	388 kcal
Fat	12.6 g
Carbohydrates	59.8g
Protein	9.6 g
Cholesterol	35 mg
Sodium	587 mg

* Percent Daily Values are based on a 2,000 calorie diet.

SHALLOTS AND CARROTS POTATO SOUP

Ingredients

- 2 tsp canola oil
- 1/2 C. chopped shallots
- 3 C. 1/2-inch cubes peeled sweet potato
- 1 1/2 C. 1/4-inch slices peeled carrot
- 1 tbsp grated fresh ginger root
- 2 tsp curry powder
- 3 C. fat free, low-sodium chicken broth
- 1/2 tsp salt

Directions

- In a large pan, heat the oil on medium-high heat and sauté the shallots for about 3 minutes.
- Stir in the sweet potato, carrot, ginger and curry powder and cook for about 3-4 minutes.
- Add the chicken broth and bring to a boil.
- Reduce the heat to low and simmer, covered for about 25-30 minutes.
- Season the soup with the salt.
- Remove from the heat and keep aside to cool slightly.

- In a blender, add the soup in batches and pulse till smooth.

Amount per serving (5 total)

Timing Information:

Preparation	15 m
Cooking	35 m
Total Time	50 m

Nutritional Information:

Calories	131 kcal
Fat	2.1 g
Carbohydrates	23.1g
Protein	5.7 g
Cholesterol	0 mg
Sodium	539 mg

* Percent Daily Values are based on a 2,000 calorie diet.

A Vegan's Potato Soup

Ingredients

- 4 large carrots, thinly sliced
- 2 large potatoes, thinly sliced
- 1 large onion, thinly sliced
- 1/4 medium head green cabbage, thinly sliced
- 2 cloves garlic, smashed
- 6 C. chicken stock
- 1 tbsp olive oil
- 1/4 tsp dried thyme
- 1/4 tsp dried basil
- 1 tsp dried parsley
- 1 tsp salt
- ground black pepper to taste

Directions

- In a large soup pan, mix together the carrots, potatoes, onion, cabbage, garlic, chicken broth, olive oil, thyme, basil, parsley, salt and pepper on medium-high heat and bring to a boil.
- Cook for about 20 minutes.
- Remove from the heat and keep aside to cool slightly.

- In a blender, add the soup in batches and pulse till smooth.

Amount per serving (6 total)

Timing Information:

Preparation	30 m
Cooking	20 m
Total Time	50 m

Nutritional Information:

Calories	161 kcal
Fat	3.1 g
Carbohydrates	31.3g
Protein	3.8 g
Cholesterol	1 mg
Sodium	1196 mg

* Percent Daily Values are based on a 2,000 calorie diet.

Seasoned Chicken and Corn Soup

Ingredients

- 2 quarts water
- 8 skinless, boneless chicken breast halves
- 1/2 tsp salt
- 1 tsp ground black pepper
- 1 tsp garlic powder
- 2 tbsps dried parsley
- 1 tbsp onion powder
- 5 cubes chicken bouillon
- 3 tbsps olive oil
- 1 onion, chopped
- 3 cloves garlic, chopped
- 1 (16 oz.) jar chunky salsa
- 2 (14.5 oz.) cans peeled and minced tomatoes
- 1 (14.5 oz.) can whole peeled tomatoes
- 1 (10.75 oz.) can condensed tomato soup
- 3 tbsps chili powder
- 1 (15 oz.) can whole kernel corn, drained
- 2 (16 oz.) cans chili beans, undrained
- 1 (8 oz.) container sour cream

Directions

- Bring a mixture of water, parsley, chicken, salt, pepper, garlic powder, onion powder and bouillon cubes to boil before cooking it over low heat for one full hour.
- Remove the chicken and shred it.
- Now cook onion and garlic in hot olive oil for a few minutes before adding salsa, minced tomatoes, whole tomatoes, tomato soup, chili powder, corn, chili beans, sour cream, shredded chicken and 5 C. broth into the pan.
- Cook on low heat for 30 minutes.
- Serve.

Serving: 8

Timing Information:

Preparation	Cooking	Total Time
15 mins	30 mins	45 mins

Nutritional Information:

Calories	473 kcal
Fat	15.3 g
Cholesterol	82 mg
Sodium	2436 mg
Carbohydrates	50.3 g
Fiber	10.1 g
Protein	39.6 g

* Percent Daily Values are based on a 2,000 calorie diet.

Spicy Kale and Onion Soup

Ingredients

- 12 links spicy pork sausage, sliced
- 1 tbsp vegetable oil
- 3/4 C. minced onion
- 1 1/4 tsps minced garlic
- 2 tbsps chicken soup base
- 4 C. water
- 2 potatoes, halved and sliced
- 2 C. sliced kale
- 1/3 C. heavy cream

Directions

- Set your oven at 300 degrees F before doing anything else.
- Bake sausage links in the preheated oven for about 25 minutes before slicing it into half inch slices.
- Cook onion and garlic in hot oil for one minute before adding broth, water, potatoes and cooking it for 14 minutes.
- Turn down the heat to low and stir in sausage, kale and cream.
- Cook for a few more minutes and serve.

Serving: 5

Timing Information:

Preparation	Cooking	Total Time
15 mins	1 hr	1 hr 15 mins

Nutritional Information:

Calories	271 kcal
Fat	21.7 g
Cholesterol	72 mg
Sodium	1216 mg
Carbohydrates	6.8 g
Fiber	1.3 g
Protein	12.4 g

* Percent Daily Values are based on a 2,000 calorie diet.

POTATOES, CORN, AND STEAK SOUP

Ingredients

- 2 tbsps butter
- 2 tbsps vegetable oil
- 1 1/2 lbs lean boneless beef round steak, cut into cubes
- 1/2 C. chopped onion
- 3 tbsps all-purpose flour
- 1 tbsp paprika
- 1 tsp salt
- 1/4 tsp ground black pepper
- 4 C. beef broth
- 2 C. water
- 4 sprigs fresh parsley, chopped
- 2 tbsps chopped celery leaves
- 1 bay leaf
- 1/2 tsp dried marjoram
- 1 1/2 C. peeled, minced Yukon Gold potatoes
- 1 1/2 C. sliced carrots
- 1 1/2 C. chopped celery
- 1 (6 oz.) can tomato paste
- 1 (15.25 oz.) can whole kernel corn, drained

Directions

- Cook steak cubes and onion in a hot mixture of butter and oil for 10 minutes before stirring in a mixture of pepper, paprika, flour and salt into the pan.
- Now add this mixture to a large pot containing a mixture of beef broth, water, celery leaves, marjoram, bay leave and parsley before cooking it for 45 minutes or until the meat is tender.
- Now stir in potatoes, tomato paste, carrots, celery and corn before cooking it over low heat for 20 more minutes or until the vegetables are tender.
- Remove bay leaf from the soup and serve.

Serving: 8

Timing Information:

Preparation	Cooking	Total Time
45 mins	1 hr 30 mins	2 hr 15 mins

Nutritional Information:

Calories	361 kcal
Fat	12.9 g
Cholesterol	84 mg
Sodium	1118 mg
Carbohydrates	26.9 g
Fiber	4.4 g
Protein	36 g

* Percent Daily Values are based on a 2,000 calorie diet.

SIMPLE SOUP

Ingredients

- 1 lb Italian sausage
- 2 onions, chopped
- 1 (28 oz.) can whole peeled tomatoes with juice
- 6 C. chicken broth
- 2 tsps dried basil
- 2 C. bow tie pasta
- 1/2 tsp garlic salt
- 1 C. chopped celery
- 1 C. chopped carrots
- 1 1/2 C. shredded cabbage

Directions

- Cook sausage until no longer pink before adding carrots, onions and celery, and cooking all this for 5 minutes.
- Bring the mixture to boil after stirring in tomatoes, cabbage, chicken broth and basil.
- Add macaroni and cook on low heat for 10 minutes before adding garlic salt.
- Serve.

Serving: 6

Timing Information:

Preparation	Cooking	Total Time
15 mins	20 mins	35 mins

Nutritional Information:

Calories	399 kcal
Fat	25.7 g
Cholesterol	58 mg
Sodium	1690 mg
Carbohydrates	23.1 g
Fiber	3.9 g
Protein	19.3 g

* Percent Daily Values are based on a 2,000 calorie diet.

SQUASH AND CILANTRO SOUP

Ingredients

- 2 cubes chicken bouillon, crumbled
- 2 C. hot water
- 1 tbsp unsalted butter
- 1 small yellow onion, minced
- 3 cloves garlic, minced
- 1/4 tsp mashed red pepper flakes
- 2 chayote squashes, peeled and cut into 1/2-inch pieces
- 2 tbsps chopped fresh cilantro
- salt and ground black pepper to taste
- 1 tbsp chopped fresh cilantro

Directions

- Cook onion, red pepper and garlic in hot butter for a few minutes and add the squash, 2 tbsps cilantro, salt, and pepper before cooking it for another 5 minutes.
- Now stir in bouillon (which was dissolved in hot water) and cilantro before cooking all this on low heat for 20 minutes.
- Blend the mixture in a blender until smooth.
- Serve in bowls.

Serving: 4

Timing Information:

Preparation	Cooking	Total Time
30 mins	30 mins	1 hr

Nutritional Information:

Calories	61 kcal
Fat	3.2 g
Cholesterol	8 mg
Sodium	604 mg
Carbohydrates	7.7 g
Fiber	2.2 g
Protein	1.6 g

* Percent Daily Values are based on a 2,000 calorie diet.

CANNELLINI AND TOMATO SOUP

Ingredients

- 1 tbsp olive oil
- 2 lbs bulk Italian sausage
- 2 (32 oz.) cartons chicken broth
- 2 (15 oz.) cans cannellini beans, rinsed and drained
- 1 head escarole, chopped
- 1 (15 oz.) can tomato sauce

Directions

- Cook sausage in hot olive oil for 10 minutes before adding chicken broth, beans, escarole, and tomato sauce into the pan.
- Cook on low heat for 20 minutes.
- Serve.

Serving: 14

Timing Information:

Preparation	Cooking	Total Time
10 mins	20 mins	30 mins

Nutritional Information:

Calories	303 kcal
Fat	19.4 g
Cholesterol	40 mg
Sodium	1688 mg
Carbohydrates	15 g
Fiber	4.3 g
Protein	16.4 g

* Percent Daily Values are based on a 2,000 calorie diet.

TURKEY LEG SOUP

Ingredients

- 2 turkey legs
- 1 C. minced celery
- 1 1/2 C. minced potatoes
- 2 (10.75 oz.) cans condensed cream of chicken soup
- 1 lb processed cheese, cubed
- 1 C. minced carrots
- 1 C. minced onion
- 1 (16 oz.) package frozen chopped broccoli
- 4 C. water

Directions

- Bring water to boil after adding turkey and cook until tender before cutting up meat and adding it back into the pot.
- Stir in onions, celery, potatoes and carrots, and cook until tender before adding frozen vegetables and cooking all this again for 15 minutes.
- Add cream of chicken soup and also some cubed cheese, and cook until the cheese melts.
- Serve.

Serving: 7

Timing Information:

Preparation	Cooking	Total Time
15 mins	1 hr 10 mins	1 hr 25 mins

Nutritional Information:

Calories	472 kcal
Fat	25.2 g
Cholesterol	146 mg
Sodium	1505 mg
Carbohydrates	24.6 g
Fiber	3.8 g
Protein	37.1 g

* Percent Daily Values are based on a 2,000 calorie diet.

SOUTH OF THE BORDER SOUP

Ingredients

- 3 cooked, boneless chicken breast halves, shredded
- 1 (15 oz.) can kidney beans
- 1 C. whole kernel corn
- 1 (14.5 oz.) can stewed tomatoes
- 1/2 C. chopped onion
- 1/2 green bell pepper, chopped
- 1/2 red bell pepper, chopped
- 1 (4 oz.) can chopped green chili peppers
- 2 (14.5 oz.) cans chicken broth
- 1 tbsp ground cumin

Directions

- Put cooked chicken, red and green bell peppers, tomatoes, kidney beans, corn, onion, chilis, broth and cumin over medium heat in large sized skillet.
- Cook everything for 45 minutes.
- Serve.

Serving: 4

Timing Information:

Preparation	Cooking	Total Time
20 mins	45 mins	1 hr 5 mins

Nutritional Information:

Calories	335 kcal
Fat	7.7 g
Cholesterol	62 mg
Sodium	841 mg
Carbohydrates	37.7 g
Fiber	9.7 g
Protein	31.5 g

* Percent Daily Values are based on a 2,000 calorie diet.

SAUERKRAUT SWISS SOUP

Ingredients

- 1/2 C. chopped onion
- 1/4 C. chopped celery
- 3 tbsps butter
- 1/4 C. all-purpose flour
- 3 C. water
- 4 cubes beef bouillon
- 8 oz. shredded corned beef
- 1 C. sauerkraut, drained
- 3 C. half-and-half cream
- 3 C. shredded Swiss cheese
- 8 slices rye bread, toasted and cut into triangles

Directions

- Cook onion and celery in hot butter for a few minutes and then add flour, bouillon and water before bringing all this to boil.
- Cook on low heat for 5 minutes and then add cream, corned beef, sauerkraut and 1 C. of the cheese before cooking everything for 30 minutes more.
- Serve in bowls after topping it with bread and cheese, and broiling it until the cheese melts.

Serving: 8

Timing Information:

Preparation	Cooking	Total Time
15 mins	1 hr	1 hr 15 mins

Nutritional Information:

Calories	465 kcal
Fat	30.5 g
Cholesterol	107 mg
Sodium	1127 mg
Carbohydrates	24.3 g
Fiber	1.7 g
Protein	24.7 g

* Percent Daily Values are based on a 2,000 calorie diet.

South of the Border Soup II

Ingredients

- 1 1/4 C. dried pinto beans
- 4 lbs pork spareribs
- 1/4 C. vegetable oil
- 1 C. chopped onion
- 2 cloves garlic, minced
- 2 (14 oz.) cans beef broth
- 4 C. water
- 2 tsps chili powder
- 1 tsp dried oregano
- 1 tsp ground cumin
- 1/2 tsp salt
- 1/4 tsp ground black pepper
- 1/4 C. chopped fresh cilantro

Directions

- Bring a mixture of rinsed beans and water to boil for 2 minutes before turning the heat off and letting it set as it is for one full hour.
- Cook onion and garlic in hot oil for 5 minutes and add beans, ground black pepper, browned ribs, salt, broth, water, cumin, chili powder, oregano, and fresh cilantro

before covering up the pan and cooking everything for 90 minutes or until you find that the meat is tender.

- Remove the meat from the bones and wait for the fat to rise up before bringing the soup back to boil and cooking it on low heat for 30 more minutes.
- Serve.

Serving: 10

Timing Information:

Preparation	Cooking	Total Time
15 mins	2 hr 30 mins	2 hr 45 mins

Nutritional Information:

Calories	651 kcal
Fat	48.6 g
Cholesterol	145 mg
Sodium	532 mg
Carbohydrates	17.4 g
Fiber	4.3 g
Protein	34.5 g

* Percent Daily Values are based on a 2,000 calorie diet.

CHICKEN SOUP (COUNTRYSIDE STYLE)

Ingredients

- 4 C. chicken broth
- 2 C. water
- 2 cooked, boneless chicken breast halves, shredded
- 1 (4.5 oz.) package quick cooking long grain and wild rice with seasoning packet
- 1/2 tsp salt
- 1/2 tsp ground black pepper
- 3/4 C. all-purpose flour
- 1/2 C. butter
- 2 C. heavy cream

Directions

- Bring a mixture of broth, chicken and water to boil and add rice before turning off the heat and covering it up.
- Cook content of seasoning packet in hot butter until bubbly before turning down the heat to low and stirring a mixture of salt, pepper and flour.
- Now add cream and cook for another 5 minutes.
- Now pour this cream mixture into the rice mixture before cooking it over medium heat for about 15 minutes.
- Serve.

Serving: 8

Timing Information:

Preparation	Cooking	Total Time
5 mins	20 mins	25 mins

Nutritional Information:

Calories	462 kcal
Fat	36.5 g
Cholesterol	135 mg
Sodium	997 mg
Carbohydrates	22.6 g
Fiber	1 g
Protein	12 g

* Percent Daily Values are based on a 2,000 calorie diet.

THANKS FOR READING! JOIN THE CLUB AND KEEP ON COOKING WITH 6 MORE COOKBOOKS....

http://bit.ly/1TdrStv

 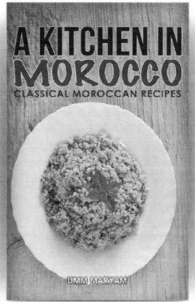 

To grab the box sets simply follow the link mentioned above, or tap one of book covers.

This will take you to a page where you can simply enter your email address and a PDF version of the box sets will be emailed to you.

Hope you are ready for some serious cooking!

http://bit.ly/1TdrStv

COME ON...
LET'S BE FRIENDS :)

We adore our readers and love connecting with them socially.

Like BookSumo on Facebook and let's get social!

Facebook

And also check out the BookSumo Cooking Blog.

Food Lover Blog

Printed in Great Britain
by Amazon